W9-CFY-109

light a candle
listen to the wind
draw a picture
eat some chocolate
open a book
look at the moon
smile at yourself

A Whimsical and Uplifting Look at Life
from the Pen and Brush
of
Kristin Sheldon

ISBN: 0-88396-436-8

⌐⌐⌐
⌐⌐ design on book cover is registered in U. S. Patent
and Trademark Office.

Manufactured in the United States of America
First Printing: February, 1996

This book is printed on fine quality, laid embossed, 80 lb. recycled paper. This paper has been specially produced to be acid free (neutral pH) and contains no groundwood or unbleached pulp. It conforms with all of the requirements of the American National Standards Institute, Inc., so as to ensure that this book will last and be enjoyed by future generations.

Blue Mountain Press ®

P. O. Box 4549, Boulder, Colorado 80306

the
world
is at
your
feet

everything
is within
reach

celebrate
something
every day

life is full
of
days to crow
flowers to grow
seasons to snow
boats to row
cars to tow
seeds to sow
weeds to hoe
lawns to mow
books to know
candles to blow

a friend is like
a quilt
designed by heart
pieced in time
sewn by hand
and bound
to keep you covered

friendship is continuous

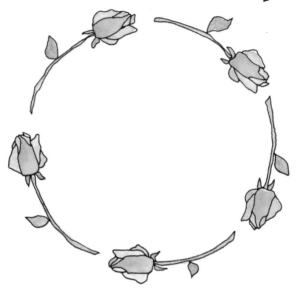

memories, blue jeans, bicycle seats and you

get better with age

with every
great loss
there springs
new life

this
too
shall
pass

you will never fly
if you don't try

the past is gone
tomorrow may come
the moment is everything

we grow together

we share
common ground

we are a garden

save some seeds
press a flower
catch a leaf
notice the clouds
plant a new tree
walk in the rain
taste a snowflake

a Staredown

share an umbrella
send a flower
call a friend
write a letter
smile at a stranger
hug someone
pick up some litter
feed the birds

never
look
back

trust the moon

hearts in sync

when you're over the hill,
you pick up speed

may you
always have
tailwinds

paws in the flowers

friends
keep you
growing

once in a while
I dig in my heels

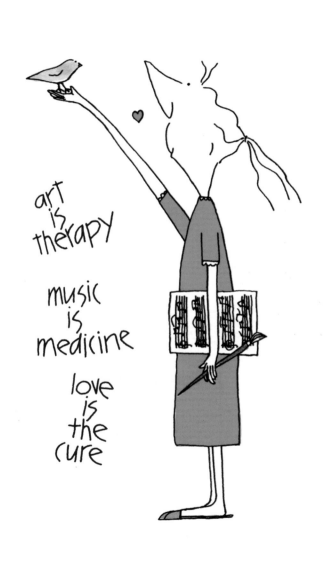

art is therapy

music is medicine

love is the cure

room
with a
view

hum and hug...
easy to spell
hard to explain
fun to share
both are free

Give peas a chance...

light a candle
listen to the wind
draw a picture
eat some chocolate
open a book
look at the moon
smile at yourself

About the Author

With her whimsical pen and watercolor drawings, Kristin Sheldon taps into the hopes, fears, and challenges that all of us share. It is her ability to see the humor inherent in human nature and common life experiences that makes her work so unique. Her playful graphics and inspirational messages tug at the strings that connect each of us with one another.

Kristin has been drawing for as long as she can remember. She has a degree in journalism from the University of Colorado, which perhaps explains her flair for creating clever twists of wordplay out of the nuances of our language. In her spare time, she enjoys gardening, fly-fishing, cycling, and hiking in the mountains near her home in Colorado where she lives with her family.

In addition to this book, Kristin's delightful illustrations can be found on **Heartstrings**® notecards and prints, also published by Blue Mountain Arts®.